MASTER DRAWINGS

Printed in the U.S.A.

MASTER DRAWINGS

Edited by

BRYAN HOLME

THE STUDIO PUBLICATIONS INCORPORATED

NEW YORK AND LONDON

"How small is the power of words to convey clear notions of visible things and on the contrary how well fitted for this task is the craft of the limner."

LEONARDO DA VINCI

INTRODUCTION

THE expression of all forms of fine and applied art starts with sketches and drawings. In this medium then we may see the graphic outline of an artist's conception of any subject, alternatively his intimate impressions taken directly from life. The sketches and drawings in museums and private collections may be the preliminary stages of the creation of a painting, fresco, etching, engraving, woodcut, tapestry, sculpture, ceramic, architecture or any other branch of art. Confronted with such a stupendous range of material it is necessary to segregate those studies which started out to be and remained essentially plans or rough sketches, with little interest except in relation to the final outcome of the artist's idea, and those studies, whether completed drawings or not, which bear a sufficient stamp of greatness to be considered, in themselves, works of art. In other words, some drawings may be no more than a quick expression of an artist's thought or perception, but others, the natural outcome of long study and work, present us with definite conclusions.

One of the chief purposes of this book being to review drawings as works of art comparable in interest to any other medium of art expression, the selection has been made with this in mind.

Before the sixteenth century drawing, generally speaking, was not considered an end in itself, but soon after the beginning of that century artists began to see in the medium a legitimate means of expression. Parmigianino (1504–1540), a pupil of Correggio (1485–1534), is the first known artist actually to make copies of his drawings. He also made offsets, woodcuts, chiaroscuro prints, and reproductive etchings through which his work became more widely known.

During the same period, in Florence, lived and worked the greatest draughtsman of the Renaissance, and probably of all time. Michelangelo (1475–1564), however, made comparatively few drawings that were not intended for his own use as studies for his sculpture, painting, or frescos. Of Da Vinci (1452–1519), his greatest rival while he yet lived, and of the younger painter, Raphael (1483–1520) the same can be said. Yet from this phenomenal trio (not to mention from the two German masters of that time, Dürer (1471–1528) and Hans Holbein the Younger (1497–1543), we have the most valuable heritage of drawings of any similar period of time or, for that matter, of any century before or since. From this it follows that we need not exclude in an appreciation of *drawings as an art* notable examples which may not actually have been intended as "show" pieces at the time they were made.

In one way the medium of drawing is more elastic than any other, for there are many combinations possible of materials as well as of technique. An artist can choose between pen and ink, (or sepia or bistre*), pencil, colored chalk, crayon of each of which there are many kinds—and charcoal. There is also pastel—though the modern technique may be said to have taken pastel out of the realm of drawing into painting. However, pastel (and chalk) is often employed to accentuate the highlights of a drawing. To this must be added metal-point, a technique mostly used by the old masters on a specially prepared surface, and the popular technique of wash which is applied with a fine brush for shading, background, solid colors or highlights. Although the most usual wash colors were grey, black, sepia (and Chinese white for heightening), other plain colors were sometimes introduced by the old masters. In the portraits by Cranach the Younger (1515–1586), Holbein the Younger, Clouet (1505–1572), and in many works by Dürer actual water colors were painted within the lines of the drawing. Although the old technique of colored brush drawings differs greatly from the modern conception of water color, the latter developed naturally from the former. A variety of water color sometimes used by Dürer in his landscapes, flowers, and animal studies was technically called *body-color*, the mixing of Chinese white with a pigment to make it opaque. There is really little difference between this and the more fashionably termed *gouache* except that studies referred to as gouache often include, with the body-color, a special mixture of gum. If besides these different materials and methods of application we consider also the parchments and textures and colors of paper available for drawings, we begin to see the endless effects that are possible within the accepted limitations of the medium.

In books of a general nature about art, the usual method of presentation is to classify the art of each country separately, starting with the earliest known works and ending with the latest. This is obviously the best way in an exhaustive study, but this book is in no sense a history; it is, precisely, a book of important drawings assembled for our appreciation and enjoyment. I prefer to arrange the artists chronologically, but not to separate them by countries. Although the external conditions of a country often influenced the fashion of an artist's work, and sometimes is the feature we like best about it, there lies beneath a great work some quality that transcends the boundaries of time or place. We can see something more in a Da Vinci head than an Italian face or headdress and something more in Dürer's drawings of hands than the hands of a German. It is from this point of view that the art of the past can be most helpful to artists today, and, in a broader sense, of more lasting interest to the connoisseur or layman. And so let us start by breaking down as many barriers as possible and ask ourselves—what is it we expect of drawings, or of any works of art? Also what is it that is similar about artists' works of the

(* *Sepia is made from the dye of cuttle fish. Bistre, also frequently used in old master drawings, was a preparation of yellow brown soot containing tar.*)

6

different periods, schools and countries? It seems to me that we can divide the past few centuries of art into five separate lines which run through all centuries, but there is one underlying principle which refers to all lines. An artist must draw, or paint, from life what he sees or feels. Therefore to the extent that all men are and always have been alike, so what he sees and feels is and always has been alike. To the extent, however, that man's personalities and perceptions differ so do his works differ. Even the most imaginative work must bear a relationship to ourselves, our functions, and to nature in general—otherwise it becomes purely intellectual or mathematical, resulting in lines, circles, squares, cubes, or formless shapes, which prove little or nothing. Abstract art may be effective from the point of view of craftsmanship or designing, but it comes in quite a different category from our present survey.

As we have touched upon the idea of imaginative drawing and painting, we may take as our first line of art the one which includes William Blake (1757–1827), probably the most imaginative draughtsman we know. In spite of this, Blake's biblical and mythological themes are based on strongly recognizable feelings and beliefs. With keen perception he attempted to represent the mystical aspect of man in relation to the universe—a broad and immensely controversial theme. Although Blake is in many respects unique, he obviously takes an important place amongst those artists who have sought primarily to express something deeper, on a higher plane, than the purely external appearance of people and things. While other artists like El Greco (1541–1614) and many of the great Renaissance artists have expressed a *psychological* side of man more subtly and with better technique than Blake, others have expressed their ideas much less profoundly.

By way of direct contrast to Blake, another great name in art is J. A. D. Ingres (1780–1867) who lived at the same time. We probably have no right to assume what Ingres' philosophy was, not knowing for certain what he may have wished to draw, but one can and must judge his work on the basis of what he has left us to see, and that is the work of a very great technician whose studies of people and figures express the worldly aspect of his subject. That is, however beautiful they may be to look at from one point of view, they are essentially photographic and obvious when compared with the work of Blake or with the work of any other artist of strong emotional feeling. Here then we have a second line—made up of artists whose work is mostly *external* and has little if any feeling for spiritual qualities. In this group also must be put those artists who render documentary sketches for purposes of information or comparison—architectural drawings or detailed drawings of birds, animals, and plant life, which we may admire for their masterful technique rather than for any other virtue.

A third line can be drawn for those artists whose chief subject interest is the life history of their particular period and locality. This they depict with fashionable aplomb, with biting satire or with genial caricature. In this category belong such artists as Pieter Breughel (1525–1569), Van Ostade (1610–1685), William Hogarth (1697–1764), François Boucher (1703–1770), J. H. Fragonard (1732–1806), Francisco Goya (1746–1828), Thomas Rowlandson (1756–1827), Constantin Guys (1805–1892), Toulouse Lautrec (1864–1901). They comprise the long line of *illustrator draughtsmen* whose work is essentially a personal document of their particular period.

In the fourth classification lie those artists whose style, as well as theme, is strongly *poetical*. In this group we can place the work of most of the great Asiatics, particularly the 16th and 17th century Persian (in their illuminated manuscripts) and on a different scale such artists as Odilon Redon (1840–1916), Eugene Berman (contemporary) and other fantasy artists whose themes have a definite poetical feeling.

The fifth logical distinction can be drawn for artists whose work in its essential form is *experimental*, but which, in some respects, represents an idea or technique clearly and importantly enough to have earned the artist the reputation of a master. Concrete examples of these artists are easiest to find in the moderns, though it is reasonable to suppose they have always existed and particularly at the initial stages of any new movement in the history of art. So accustomed are we now to the result of past deviation in technique, that for the most part we forget the long experimental period which existed between one ultimate achievement and the next. In many cases little or no documentary evidence of the actual struggle is left us to see. For instance, there are no drawings extant of Cimabue (1240?–1301) or Duccio (1255–1319), and none that can be safely attributed to Giotto (1276–1336), who is popularly called the father of European art. On the other hand we have all the evidence we need of Paul Cézanne (1839–1906) who stands in the same position to modern art as Giotto did to the Italian Renaissance. Whether Cézanne's work, or merely his influence, will live through the centuries is a question we must leave to the theorists, or better still, to posterity. Obviously we cannot see the same conclusion in Cézanne as we can in Giotto, though at the time Giotto worked he undoubtedly created as much disturbance among his contemporaries as Cézanne did amongst his. The feud between Byzantine art, and the *new art* continued for a long time in Italy. Cézanne and Vincent Van Gogh (1853–1890) were, and Pablo Picasso is, to say the least, revolutionary. To the majority of people much of their work and the work of other moderns still needs explanation. Being important enough at least for a certain amount of explanation, these and other artists of an experimental genre must fall into a separate category.

An obvious looseness appears in a general classification of this nature. Many sub-divisions can be made, and there are artists whose work may be said to be evenly balanced between two or more categories—nevertheless one can establish definite values along these lines. Knowing the characteristic ingredients, so to speak, we can decide the type of recipe which interests us most. This is the best way I know of approaching art as a whole and may help to prevent the habit many people have of considering art something apart from their daily life because they think they cannot understand it. There is no reason for placing art on a revered pedestal, no reason for separating it from anything else we see and choose to have around us, for there must be at least one line that corresponds to our own particular taste if we stop for a moment to analyze and choose.

The drawings I have included in this limited survey are representative of the best of each period and though very many of the great masterpieces are necessarily excluded because of space, there are enough to give one a general picture—the flavor of each period, the characteristic of each style, so that we may review the differences and similarities, the greatnesses and weaknesses of the different masters in relation to each other and the history of drawing as a whole.

There is a greater analogy, generally speaking, between artists' drawings of each century than there is between their work in any other medium. The reason for this is clear if we remember that so many drawings were routine studio sketches or, as was mentioned earlier in this introduction, were preliminary studies for painting, sculpture, or fresco. As such, they seldom reached the high degree of finish which particularly distinguishes one artist's technique from another. By this I do not mean that it is not easy to distinguish at first glance a Rubens from a Boucher drawing, but I do mean that the closer to the fundamental structure of art we come, the greater the analogies we find—and the same principle holds good for any subject we study. What is also interesting here is that by looking at the sketches still existing of many of the old masters we begin to see how the effectiveness of unfinished line influenced the moderns to adopt this formula as an end in itself, not only for drawing but for painting as well. So often the spontaneity of a quickly rendered sketch and the accidental qualities that appear in it are well nigh impossible to retain in a perfectly finished study. Only the greatest masters of all manage to express the flowing movement and emotional quality of line with a solidity that makes the work convincing, beautiful, and of lasting worth. Although, as an artist recently remarked to me, the wonderful part of a sketch is that it has a *future*, it is the common weakness of modern painters to place too much reliance on the accidental quality of draughtsmanship or painting to achieve their effects. By that I mean that chance should not be a guiding principle. It is true that an artist like Rembrandt (1606–1669) made the maximum use of drawing as a light and free medium of expression, but his genius *and* his conscience could not allow him to leave this as the only record of his work. Rembrandt, in other words, could compete with the most modern draughtsmen in the impressionist use of pencil and wash, but I question the ability of most moderns to compete, if they wanted to, with Rembrandt's technique in oils. An artist must have a basic training before he can, at will, indulge in fancies, and he cannot continually make a virtue out of mistakes. But here the term modern has been used too loosely, for there are many living artists whose painting in the final analysis may well stand the test of time—and time is really the only reliable critic we have. We must remember that fifty years in the history of art is small compared to the whole, and that very few great names emerge from the receding years of any but the greatest periods. Even then the number is very small compared to those which have, after a brief flash, fallen back into obscurity. How many Michelangelos are there? How many El Grecos? Accepting the inevitable answer to such a question, we are forced to make room for the works of art by men of lesser stature, some of whose works appeal equally to one or more sides of our particular taste. A reverence for one particular artist or school should not exclude an appreciation of another. Because one is awed by a Tintoretto (1518–1594) masterpiece, it should not exclude the enjoyment of Guys, or because one's favorite artist is Pisanello (1397–1455) we might not, in a different way, also like the contemporary drawings of Matisse.

Although this book resolved itself into a collection of European drawings, I have included works by Persian artists of the sixteenth and seventeenth centuries because I believe that any general survey of western drawings covering these particular centuries should at least touch upon the genius of these near Eastern artists. The exquisite detail of line, the perfect proportion, and the sheer lyrical quality of this work has given much to Europe in the past and will always carry an important message to the contemporary artist anywhere. It may be argued that, on this basis, Chinese drawings should also be included. If space permitted, there would be no reason to exclude them, except that Far Eastern art has been a less direct influence on Europe than Persian art has, and covering as it does such an enormous period of time, should certainly be treated as a subject on its own.

In conclusion I would say that it is our misfortune that so few important drawings exist of some of the greatest and most prolific painters of the Titian, Giorgione, Greco, Velazquez calibre, and again of many of the impressionists and our best known contemporaries. In the case of these old masters, the value of drawings, apart from their use as working sketches, was not considered, and in the case of most of the impressionists and contemporary painters, the stress has been on color rather than form—with the result that we have had, until now, comparatively little modern draughtsmanship at all comparable to the works of the past. For the most part the technique of the sketch has gone into the painting itself.

INDEX

13

1. COSTUME STUDIES. Pen, bistre and water color. PISANELLO. Veronese. XVTH Century.

2. RIVER GOD AND HORSE'S HEAD. Chalk and wash drawing. PISANELLO. Veronese

3. ANIMAL STUDIES. Chalk and pen and bistre with wash. LOMBARD SCHOOL.

4. YOUNG WOMAN. Pen, bistre, wash. FILIPPO LIPPI. Florentine. XVTH Century.

5. PORTRAIT OF A MAN. Silverpoint drawing. DIRK BOUTS. Flemish. XVᴛʜ Century.

6. STUDY OF A KNEELING LADY.   Pen and bistre.   FLEMISH.   XVᴛʜ Century.

FIGURE OF ADAM.   Charcoal, pen and wash.   POLLAJUOLO.   Florentine.   XVᴛʜ Century.

8. KNIGHT IN FANTASTIC COSTUME.　Pen and bistre.　GERMAN.　XVᴛʜ Centu

9. UMPIRES AND SPECTATORS AT A TOURNAMENT.   Pen.   JACOPO BELLINI.
Venetian. XVᴛʜ Century.

10. PORTRAIT STUDY. Chalk. GIOVANNI BELLINI. Venetian. XVᴛʜ Century.

11. HEAD OF A WOMAN. Chalk, bistre with white. VERROCCHIO. Florentine. XVᴛʜ Century.

12. APOSTLES. Brush drawing, heightened with white. MANTEGNA. Paduan. XVᴛʜ Century.

13. ST. LAURENCE.   Silverpoint, with white.   PERUGINO.   Umbrian.   XVᴛʜ Century.

14. WITCHES. Pen, wash, heightened with white. BOTTICELLI. Florentine. XVᴛʜ Century.

15. **ABUNDANCE.**   Pen and bistre, heightened with white.   **BOTTICELLI.**   Florentine.

16. ISABELLA D'ESTE.   Black chalk and pastel.   DA VINCI.   Florentine.   XVᴛʜ Century.

17. MARY MAGDALENE.   Chalk drawing.   DA VINCI.   Florentine.   XVᴛʜ Century.

18 HEAD OF CHRIST.   Chalk and tempera.   DA VINCI.   Florentine.   XVᴛʜ Century.

19. STUDY OF A HEAD.   Chalk drawing.   DA VINCI.   Florentine.   XVᴛʜ Century.

20. MADONNA AND CHILD. Pen. FRA BARTOLOMMEO. Florentine. XVᴛʜ Century.

21. STUDY FOR A ST. SEBASTIAN AND A YOUNG MAN.   Silverpoint, wash, heightened
with white. FILIPPINO LIPPI. Florentine. XVᴛʜ Century.

22. CHRIST ON THE MOUNT.   Pen and wash.   PALMA.   Venetian.   XVITH Century.

23. MADONNA AND CHILD. Pen and bistre. DI COSIMO. Florentine. XVIth Century.

24. DRAWING FOR THE HISTORY OF ST. URSULA. Pen and chalk. CARPACCIO.
Venetian. XVITH Century.

25. HOLY TRINITY.   Pen drawing.   DÜRER.   German.   XVIᵗʰ Century.

26. STUDY FOR ADAM.   Pen drawing.   DÜRER.   German.   XVITH Century.

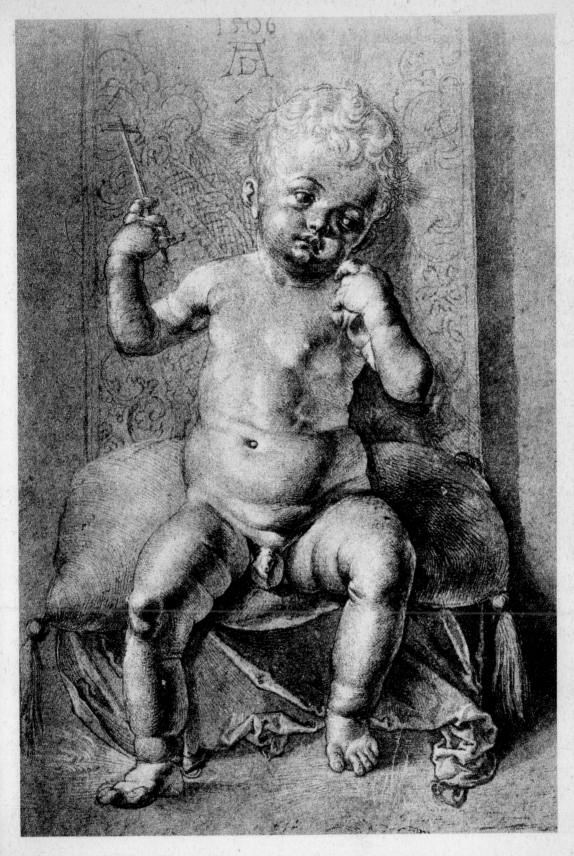

27. THE CHRISTCHILD.　Pen with wash.　DÜRER.　German.　XVIᴛʜ Century.

28. NUREMBERG GIRL. Pen with water color. **DÜRER.** German. **XVITH** Century.

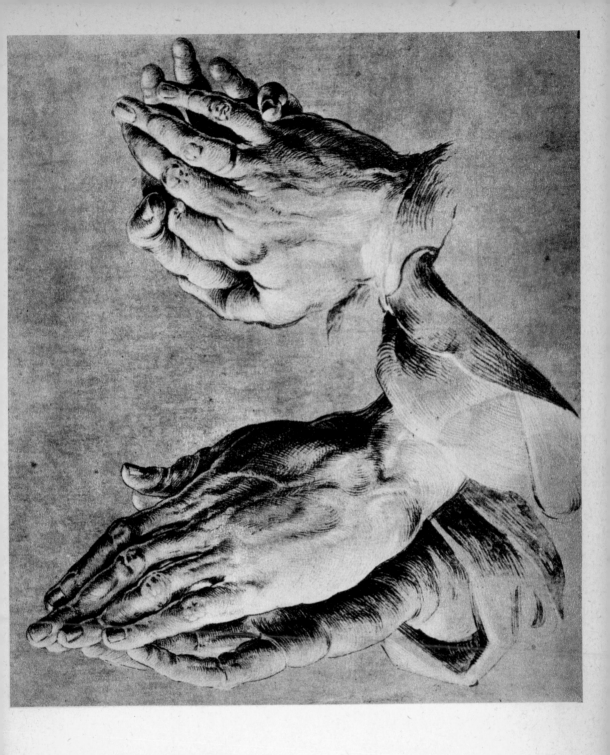

29. STUDY OF HANDS.   Pen with wash.   DÜRER.   German.   XVIᴛʜ Century.

30. THE HARE.   Pen and wash.   DÜRER.   German.   XVITH Century.

31. COLUMBINE.　　Water color drawing.　　DÜRER.　　German.　　XVITH Century.

32. HOLY FAMILY.   Silverpoint.   RAPHAEL.   Umbrian.   XVITH Century.

33. YOUNG GIRL. Black chalk heightened with white. RAPHAEL. Umbrian.

34. YOUNG WOMAN IN FRONT OF A WINDOW. Pen drawing. RAPHAEL. Umbrian

35. THREE GRACES.   Red chalk.   RAPHAEL.   Umbrian.   XVITH Century.

36. ARCHERS SHOOTING. Red chalk. MICHELANGELO. Florentine. XVIᵀᴴ Century.

37. STUDY OF CHRIST RISEN FROM THE TOMB.   Black chalk.   MICHELANGELO.

38. HEAD OF A YOUNG WOMAN.   Red chalk.   MICHELANGELO.   Florentine.
XVITH Century.

39. STUDY FOR THE LIBYAN SIBYL.　　Red chalk.　　**MICHELANGELO.**　　Florentine.

40. STUDIES OF A MADONNA AND CHILD. Pen and brown ink. MICHELANGELO.
Florentine. XVITH Century.

41. PORTRAIT OF A YOUNG WOMAN.   Red chalk.   PONTORMO.   Florentine.
XVITH Century.

42. SAINT CATHERINE. Black and red chalk. PARMIGIANINO. Italian. XVIth Century.

43. HEAD OF A BEARDED MAN. Black chalk. BANDINELLI. Florentine. XVIᵗʰ Century.

44. LANDSCAPE.   Pen and bistre.   TITIAN   (Campagnola).   Venetian.   XVIth Century.

45. THE LAST SUPPER. Wash drawing. TINTORETTO. Venetian. XVITH Century.

Clinton.

46. CLINTON. Black chalk. HOLBEIN THE YOUNGER. German. XVITH Century.

47. SIR JOHN GODSALVE.   Black chalk.   HOLBEIN THE YOUNGER.   German.

48. A WOMAN STANDING.   Pen and wash.   HOLBEIN THE YOUNGER.   German.

49. ELISABETH OF SAXONY. Pen and water color. CRANACH. German. XVITH Century.

Monfieur de lorraine
eftant petit

50. CHARLES II. Chalk with water color. FRANÇOIS CLOUET. French. XVITH Century.

51. MARGUERITE OF FRANCE. Water color drawing. FRANÇOIS CLOUET. French.

52. A VILLAGE RIVER WITH BOATS AND A PIER.   Pen and bistre touched with blue.
PIETER BREUGHEL. Flemish. XVITH Century.

53. SUMMER.   Pen and bistre.   PIETER BREUGHEL.   Flemish.   XVItH Century.

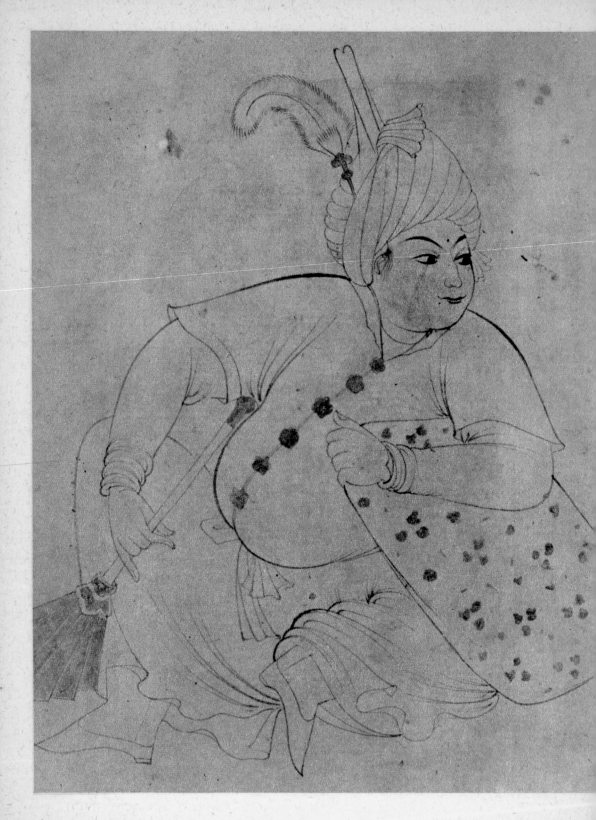

54. A COURT DWARF.   Pencil drawing.   PERSIAN.   XVIᵗʰ Century.

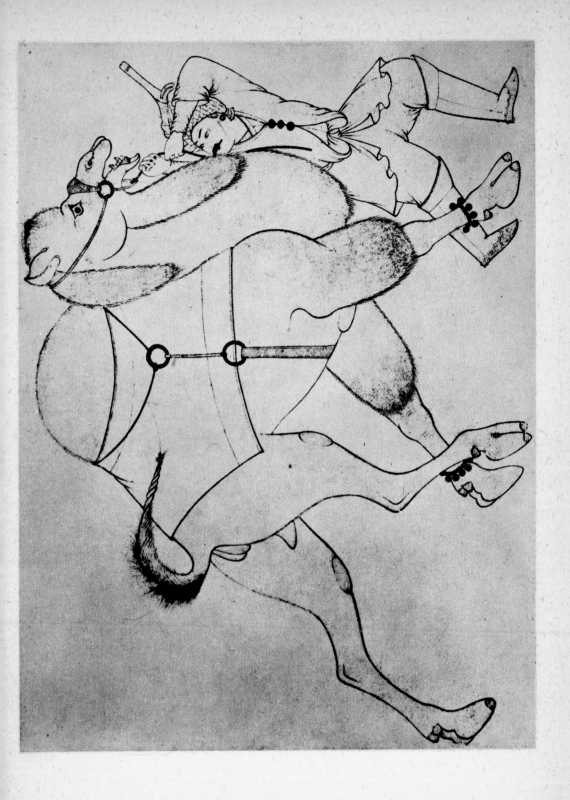

55. CAMEL WITH DRIVER.   Pen.   PERSIAN.   XVIth Century.

56. A KNEELING YOUTH.   Pen drawing.   PERSIAN.   XVIᴛʜ Century.

57. PORTRAIT OF A EUROPEAN.   Drawing with wash.   PERSIAN.   XVIIᴛʜ Century.

58. JACOB ASLEEP. Pen, bistre and wash. CARRACCI. Bolognese. XVITH Century.

59. HEAD OF A WOMAN IN THE ESPOLIO. Pen. EL GRECO. Spanish. XVITH Century.

60 PIAZZA WITH FIREWORKS.   Pen and wash.   GUERCINO.   Bolognese.

61. RUINS. Pen and brown ink. GUERCINO. Bolognese. XVIITH Century.

62. HARBOR SCENE.   Brush drawing.   JAN BREUGHEL.   Flemish.   XVIITH Century.

63. LANDSCAPE. Wash drawing. RUBENS. Flemish. XVIITH Century.

64. THE ARCHDUKE ALBERT. Pen and wash. RUBENS. Flemish. XVIITH Century.

5. MARIE DE MEDICI.　　Black chalk.　　· RUBENS.　　Flemish.　　XVIITH Century.

66. RUBENS' SON NICHOLAS. Black and red chalk. RUBENS. Flemish. XVIITH Century.

67. TWO ENGLISH HERALDS. Chalk drawing. VAN DYCK. Flemish. XVIITH Century.

the Count of Arenberg by Vandyke

68. COUNT ALBERT OF ARENBERG. Pen. VAN DYCK. Flemish. XVIITH Century.

69. THE ASSUMPTION OF THE VIRGIN. Pen. MURILLO. Spanish. XVIITH Century.

70. ESTHER AND MORDECAI. Pen and wash. REMBRANDT. Dutch. XVIITH Century.

71. WOMAN CARRYING A CHILD.   Pen, bistre and wash.   REMBRANDT.   Dutch.

72. YOUNG GIRL'S TOILET.   Pen, bistre and wash.   REMBRANDT.   Dutch.

73. INTERIOR WITH BOORS.   Pen, sepia and wash.   VAN OSTADE.   Dutch.
XVIIᴛʜ Century.

74. FLOWERS.   Wash drawing.   VAN HUYSUM.   Dutch.   XVIIITH Century.

75. LUTE PLAYER.   Chalk, with white.   PIAZZETTA.   Venetian.   XVIIITH Century.

77. CIRCULAR CHURCH. Pen and grey wash. CANALETTO. Venetian. XVIIItH Century.

78. BOAR HUNT.　　Pen, bistre and wash.　　TIEPOLO.　　Venetian.　　XVIIITH Century.

79. ABRAHAM VISITED BY THE ANGELS.   Pen, bistre and blue crayon.   TIEPOLO.
Venetian.   XVIIITH Century.

BEER STREET

80. BEER STREET.   Red chalk.   HOGARTH.   English.   XVIIITH Century.

81. LADY IN ORIENTAL COSTUME.   Chalk.   BOUCHER.   French.   XVIIITH Century.

82. RECLINING FIGURE.   Colored chalk.   BOUCHER.   French.   XVIIITH Century.

83. VILLA D'ESTE.   Water color drawing.   FRAGONARD.   French.   XVIIITH Century.

84. GRAND CANAL, VENICE. Pen and wash. GUARDI (follower). Venetian. XVIIItH Century.

85. GRAND CANAL, VENICE.   GUARDI.   Venetian.   XVIIITH Century.   Pen and wash.

86. STUDY OF A LADY.　　Black and white chalk.　　GAINSBOROUGH.　　English.

87. LANDSCAPE. Black and white chalk. GAINSBOROUGH. English. XVIIITH Century.

88. FIGURE.   Brush drawing.   ROMNEY.   English.   XVIIITH Century.

89. A GAMING TABLE. Pen and water color. ROWLANDSON. English. XVIIITH Century.

90. THE SWING.   Brush drawing.   GOYA.   Spanish.   XVIIITH Century.

91. THE STABBING.　　Brush drawing.　　GOYA.　　Spanish.　　XVIIITH Century.

92. THE GUILLON-LETHIERE FAMILY.   Pencil.   INGRES.   French.   XIXTH Century.

93. A LADY AND A BOY.   Pencil.   INGRES.   French.   XIXᴛʜ Century.

94. WOMAN TAKEN IN ADULTERY.   Water color drawing.   BLAKE.   English.

95. THE FLIGHT INTO EGYPT. Pen and water color. BLAKE. English. XIXTH Century.

96. ANGEL OF THE REVELATION. Pen and water color. BLAKE. English. XIXTH Century.

97. JOB'S EVIL DREAMS.   Pen and water color.   BLAKE.   English.   XIXᴛʜ Century.

98. ITALIAN LANDSCAPE. Pen and wash over chalk. GERICAULT. French. XIXTH Century

9. HENRY LEROY AS A CHILD. Pencil on cardboard. COROT. French. XIXᴛʜ Century.

100 LADY DRESSED FOR A BALL. Pen and brush. GUYS. French. XIXTH Century.

101 OFFICERS OF THE GUARD. Pen, ink and water color. GUYS. French. XIXTH Century.

102. HAMLET.　Water color drawing.　DELACROIX.　French.　XIXth Century.

103. THE MARKET.   Charcoal and water color.   DAUMIER.   French.   XIXTH Century.

104. A CLOWN.   Charcoal and water color.   DAUMIER.   French.   XIXᴛʜ Century.

105. EDOUARD MANET.　　Pencil drawing.　　DEGAS.　　French.　　XIXᴛʜ Century.

106. BALLET DANCERS RESTING. Pastel drawing. DEGAS. French. XIXTH Century.

107. ACHILLE EMPERAIRE. Charcoal drawing. CEZANNE. French. XIXᴛʜ Century.

108. SAIL BOATS AT HONFLEUR.　Pen and ink.　MONET.　French.　XIXTH Century.

109. CAFE SCENE.　　Pen and ink.　　MANET.　　French.　　XIXTH Century.

110. PORTRAIT OF DIETERLE. Lithographic drawing. RENOIR. French. XIXTH Century.

111. THE ARTIST IN HIS STUDIO. Black crayon. SEURAT. French. XIXTH Century.

112. LADY FISHING.   Black crayon.   SEURAT.   French.   XIXTH Century.

113. PROFILE OF A WOMAN. Chalk and pastel. REDON. French. XIXᴛʜ Century.

114. ORPHEUS.   Pastel drawing.   REDON.   French.   XIXᴛʜ Century.

115. OLD MAN WITH BOWED HEAD. Black crayon, touched with white. VAN GOGH.
Dutch. XIXTH Century.

116. WOMAN MEDITATING. Black lead and ink. VAN GOGH. Dutch. XIXTH Century.

117. CORNFIELD.   Reed pen and ink.   VAN GOGH.   Dutch.   XIXᴛʜ Century.

118. AT THE CIRCUS.   Chalk drawing.   LAUTREC.   French.   XIXTH Century.

119. PORTRAIT OF A LADY.   Pen and ink.   MATISSE.   French.   XXTH Century.

120. WHITE PLUMES.　　Pencil drawing.　　MATISSE.　　French.　　XXᴛʜ Century.

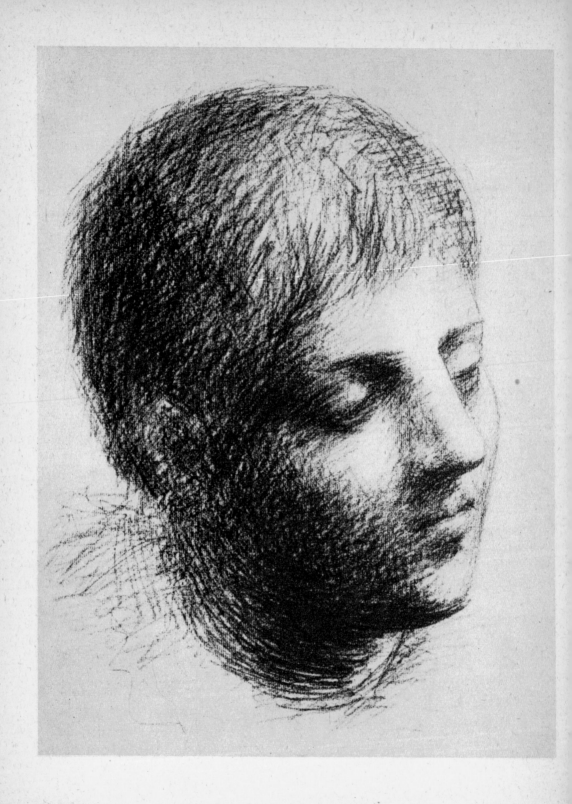

121. HEAD OF A YOUNG MAN.   Black crayon.   PICASSO.   Spanish.   XXᴛʜ Century

122. CONCERT.   Pen and ink.   **PICASSO.**   Spanish.   **XXTH Century.**

123. THREE DANCERS RESTING.   Pen and ink.   PICASSO.   Spanish.   XXᴛʜ Century.

124. FARM HAND.   Pen and wash.   **TCHELITCHEW.**   Russian.   **XXᴛʜ Century.**

125. LANDSCAPE.   Pen and ink.   DUFY.   French.   XXᴛʜ Century.

126. ANTHROPOMORPHIC ECHO.   Pen and ink.   DALI.   Spanish.   XXTH Century.

127. MOTHER AND CHILD. Colored chalk. VERTES. Hungarian. XXTH Century.

128. MUSIC.   Brush drawing.   BERMAN.   French.   XXTH Century.

129. FINETTE.　Lithographic drawing.　LAURENCIN.　French.　XXᴛʜ Century.